THE ANGRY WOODCUTTER

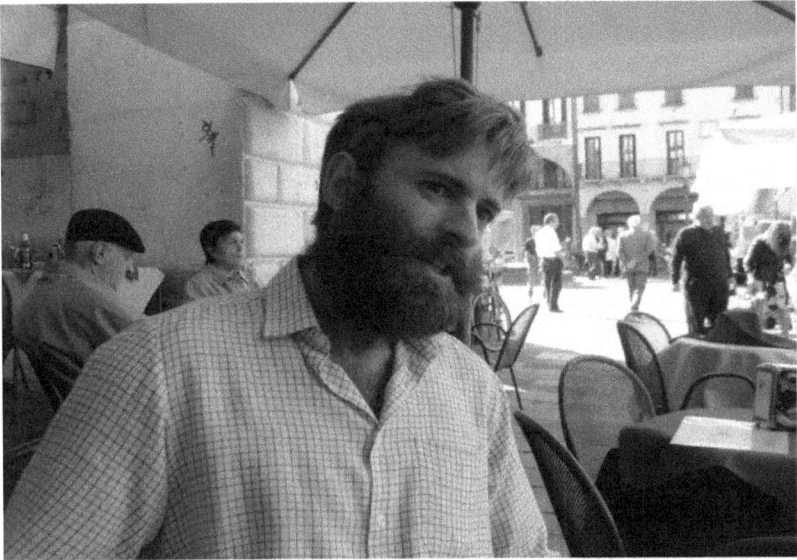

COLLECTION

Chris Deakins

Cover Photo: Author in Padova
Photo reprinted with permission from Richard Panting.

Acknowledgements are due to the editors of: 'The Journal' and 'Purple Patch' magazines, in which some of these poems have appeared.

Introduction

Christopher George Deakins:
Born 1973, son of two teachers, Father also an artist, as was Grandfather- George Deakins – oil paintings with pallete knife. One sister, born 1971.

Studied English at 'A' level, discovered works of: T.S.Eliot, Pinter, Beckett, and became avid reader of classics. Major influences include Dostoyevsky, Conrad, Henry James, Hemingway, J. Updike.

Graduated in Forestry, Bangor, N. Wales, 1996. Worked in Scotland and Norway. Forestry Contractor in Somerset from 1997. Poetry published in several magazines from 2000. Also a collection of poems: 'In a Parallel World' published 2011 as a chapbook by original plus.'Angry Woodcutter' poems first appeared in 2007.

'Angry Woodcutter'

Writing poetry helps me to process opinions, ironies, emotions. It has been suggested that I keep my angst and psychological battering to myself. I tried. The first 'Angry Woodcutter' – It's Just Bollocks - was more a reaction to working for the Forestry Commission than any wider social commentary, though a sense of the marginalised producer in a rapidly technologising, wasteful and hedonistic/consumerist society still pertains. The limitations of 'Angry Woodcutter' are not the number of chips he has on his shoulders, which I quite enjoy, and find almost Hemingwayesque, but the sheer blank refusal to engage with the cruel and simple and unavoidable truth of the economic reality of supply and demand. Angry Woodcutter rejects its profane cry.

A friend suggested I put all my 'Angry Woodcutter' poems together. I think he thought I might be able to dispense with them in that way. In a way he was right; I write fewer poems from that invented persona these days, and more about pheasants. I am including some poems which I feel are in a similar vein. I think Richard Jeffries, Thomas Hardy and John Steinbeck were writing from a similar place. But nowhere, I think, has it been written <u>from</u> the woodcutter, who appears, in many novels, as taciturn. Having known many woodcutters, that taciturnity sticks, but almost always runs alongside a deep and dry humour.

I have included the poem 'Competition' mostly in answer to the increasingly shrill call of: 'But it's a competitive world.' Selfishness, I think, by some rule of paradox, tends towards a negation of self. And I agree with Mark Twain when he says: 'Never trust a profession which requires smart clothes.'

Contents

How to be a Predator

Tired of being a slave?
Had enough of being humble? Are you one of the many...
Producing what everyone needs, but no one values?

Struggling to keep the weight on?
While a fat, idle, complacent, parasitic, diminished
responsibility 'civilisation' watches you
Through flesh tinted spectacles?
          Seen one too many overweight survival experts
march across your paddy fields? Sold your last camel
to pay for antidepressants?
Looking for an alternative to joining the Taliban?

Here it is!
If you want to find out how to feed yourself and your
family with a *minimum of effort*
Follow our step by step guide to:
Putting on weight without working.
          We'll show you *(among other things)* **how and
          where**
To find high fat meat
Ideal for winter
We'll show you
How to set up a cover trade *(need not be profitable)* **and**
How and where to set up traps to harvest the gullible
          And, importantly, we'll help you
to familiarise yourself
With 'being a predator' – an attitude and philosophy

you may not be familiar with.

By the end of the series you will understand
How your behaviour contributes towards natural selection
Via lessons such as: 'The Society Delusion' and 'The
Selfish Altruist.'

We'll also show you: how to take the upper edge
of predation –
To predate the predators,
when the market for primary consumers
Dries up or becomes too risky.
You will learn **how to get out**
And where to go in an extreme predatory environment.
For example:
Banks
Can be a safe haven when the streets
are running with blood...

All this and more in our 13 issue
'How to be a Predator' learning course.
Western experts have been studying urban predators
for years. Their knowledge has been drawn
from numerous texts and first hand accounts.

*You may be asking yourself: why am I volunteering this
profitable information
So cheaply? Let me tell you, once, I've been using these
skills for years already;
My larder is full and would feed me for a thousand
lifetimes.*
I have no more need of flesh.
But I still hanker for the hunt.

Though my body is aged my desire to kill is unquenchable.
I wish to educate some worthy 'disciples' to take on the baton
Of this important, and environmentally necessary career.

Subscribe now to: 'How to be a Predator'
And receive your first three issues free...
    Concessions
And translations available.

Angry Woodcutter: It's Just Bollocks

The problem is it's all in my mind.
The problem is it's all words. Words!
     It's a question of attitude –
Yours and mine
It's absurd
It's all so so wrong is the problem
That I can't even begin. Might as well not speak
Just vote with my feet
Like the others

PHEASANT CONVENTION

San-saens requiem – you heard it?
No.
You? Yes, fantastic, heard it
From the Langley's back garden last night
Sublime.
Not a well known piece though?
No, but none the worst for it.
Is it like Faure's or Durufle's?
Neither, it's got pathos, real pathos
And it's storming. Unfortunately I missed the last movement
cos their cat spotted me through the window and came
prowling out pretty sharp. Wild one that tabby. It's got
Exmoor Beast written all over it. Don't want to mess with the
Langley's cat. Oh_no. Harry was never the same after their
scuffle. The cat lost an ear, but Harry partially lost the use of
one wing. He was always flying into the sides of buildings
after that.

Angry Woodcutter: Digging in Poland

I've been digging in Poland...
Trying to find answers
To incomplete questions
About commerce
And waste

There is an advancement -
From Cornwall or the midlands
Idle towers, factories, towns...

An innovation –
A grinding down
By silent hypocritic conspiratorial greed.

It's a shifting, a making, a breaking
Of promises. It's confidence
And the value of the pound.
            We'll be saying: "Is it fair
To take work from the poorest?"

I've been digging
up questions about sovereignty and investment.
Because I didn't want to get left behind

Lorries scream past a man my age
Ploughing his strip of field.
Shoulders and hands heavy
As the horses breath.

In this is a balancing of everyone's futures
But with overwieldy scales –
With each tip a new wasteland forms
And an old one blackens:

Romania, Bulgaria, Ukraine, Russia
Because it's cheaper.
Are we ready to face the wheel of karma?

But here, just now, is something my finger won't touch -
An old grey shell... leaking,
Protruding by the road just here.
And those old men sitting -
Musing the dug up field - know
But won't tell.

From Galaxy 12
To Earth

Returning cosmic angst call
Your time: early revelations period.
Hi.

Angry Woodcutter: Just a Job

I should be making a contribution today.
To humanity. A camel!
Doing something productive.
Keeping timber affordable
And the world grows?

The race
Is not to win a market
It is to feed all the market
To outstrip demand, outstrip waste
Is this it?
Is this what god sent me here for?
To reduce inflation?

My morale is low.

There's a skills shortage apparently.
Why doesn't the market then do its job? Fill that gap!
Supply rising to meet demand.
It's not fast enough!

None of them are ever coming back
And not because it's dirty or dangerous
That isn't why they were *so* pissed off.

No, the market is like a Polish road...
Which is why the *industry* needs an *injection*!...

Old man, I've been wanting to tell you about it for years:
The future...I don't know whether it was machismo,
martyrdom...
Yeah. all those –
The roles of man...

Being part of something.
Was why I never joined.

                    Maps
Every millimetre compart-mentalised:
Heritage, conservation, community. Please:
Teach me other words.

Perhaps it will end.
Perhaps
I'll be taking alms
At the gates of the colony.
Better that than say I liked them.

Diary Of A Pheasant

How kind they've been. What are we –
Pecking and gobbling
When they're so caring?
        Fed us, sheltered us, saved us
From how many predators?

"They have merely kept us
For their own reasons."
        But why?
They must love us to have gone to such effort –
They're so careful over us…

Harry's dead, and Henry, I saw them fall,
And who are these people?
Where are our protectors?
We must fly for they are coming with sticks and dogs.

I am hit, being carried in sharp white teeth,
Can't feel my wings anymore,
Don't understand, for there are all my friends
Hung up in that pick-up.

But no, that pick-up is familiar. And that landrover, and that
jacket.
These hands are familiar,
These are the same hands that held me when I was cold and
afraid.
They have come at last to save me
Save me
Oh thank-you, thank-you grey eyes.

Angry Woodcutter: Today I've Retired!

I'm a bit young
But that doesn't reflect the way I feel
And I'm making my contribution
By sharing my experience!
      For the sake of argument
We'll call this liaison
Though you know me not
      And the result..?

Change
Any change
Even a minutesimal change
Is a visible result.
For example: this may encourage you,
Ask for non-certified timber.
Don't worry about a risk assessment for that
It's in the post.

So
                Today
Going out – tick
A gentle stroll - tick
To the field across the river
And into the trees. Tick
Past that clearfell that never got replanted – cross
Why didn't they spend the money on trees instead of logos?
Cross.

Nevermind. I may sit by the river
Do some sums.

Being self-employed, you see, has its advantages.
No one notices

When you go on strike –
Must be working for someone else,
Can't have retired. Couldn't. Surely…

Angry Woodcutter at Bristol airport

Good evening ladies and gentlemen
thankyou for waiting

on behalf of BMI Regional we wish you a pleasant flight.
Passengers on – thankyou for waiting
on behalf of – all passengers – we wish you
will passengers – please proceed immediately
failure to – may result in you missing your flight
we wish you – thankyou for waiting – please
even if you are regular travellers
pay attention. Breathe normally
in the unlikely event – fasten like this,
pull down and blow – don't forget to -
and have a pleasant flight
on behalf of – we wish you – on behalf of – we wish you
on behalf of – we wish you
on behalf of – we wish you -

Fear and Faith

Alarms of invasion: S.T.Coleridge, Fears in Solitude

Even if it's not what you call poetry
It's timeless, as solitude is timeless.
      As the brooding heart
And the world's undetermined conflicts,
Because of providence. We have offended.
      The callings.. The words..
All those speech mouthings
Belong anywhere, in any time,
But especially here,
On these green hills

With their flock:
The greasy politicians,
The fat controllers:
Beneficent, implacable, sensual;
The lazy farmers, juggling charms, bartering freedoms
For grants, sustainable grants, fratricide grants;
The lazy workers, the skilled, the de-motivated
All implicated in collateral damage,
All hypocrites
Complicit,
Mouthing
      Cheap and dainty words scribed against hunger
For posterity.

Poems

Poems! Poems!!
Poems about poems!
Poems about people
Who write poems
On wet days -
Poems in the rain.
Poems that never end.
Poems to remember,
Make you remember
What it's like
To feel something!
No. Not those kind of poems.

Angry Woodcutter: Working Her Out

Today I've been listening to my head
The world has been -
Green, steep
And dry.

I followed the contours,
Slipped occasionally,
Didn't fall far into bramble.

The pain was superficial,
A relief.

Thinking of you
As a crazed megalomanic bitch
Has been a relief.

Getting it Right Twice

I was your man on the outside
We were working for the same side
And both knew
The lines of trees in the sun.

So much so we almost forgot
It was work.
      Forgot too about the castle walls
Which meant I didn't have to be grateful
Somehow. Neither did you.

Angry Woodcutter: Customer

You who I love and work for.
        I want to serve you.

Tell me:
When the Commission has sold
The last of its best trees
To feed its loss,

When there are no more jobs for the boys
Or girls,
        When there's no more dole…
And the rates go back down
Tell me
I can be your butler -
Your head butler;
I'll be professional!

Somewhere A Penny Drops

Can't remember her tits.
Adored them.
Can't remember them.

Her smell. A nothing smell now.
No words for it. Nice.
Even as I try to concentrate on her crotch
which, again,
I know I went there.
It wasn't dark...
It was neither dark nor light,
more young than old.
Perhaps the smell was old, like a house
As a child.

None of it helps, the concentrating. All I can say
Charming.
        Laura's smell, on the other hand,
Earth,
An old barn
full of horse shit, and sweat. Latin sweat
Tempered by damp moss.
        Garlic hanging by the door,
straw
old fashioned meadows.
        Through the door also
blast of salt spray
hint of thyme.

Angry Woodcutter at Oslo International Airport

World Population 6.8 billion plus the unrecorded.
Population Norway 4 million.

Takes a while for the gate number to show on the screens.
It's a square tube that you look down
It's shiny, smells of factories
And the way forward and the way back
Are the same.
                    All I can see are the Alta mountains.

But there's plenty to look at.
Everyone is looking and everyone is scared
Even the seasoned   in conversation   but
Watching shadows glide along walls –
Diamond, gold;
Like there are cars outside
You can almost see the light
Through brown, chocolate brown
Nobody paints their fingernails brown

But it's a tunnel
A dull blue tunnel that absorbs sound;
Shoes, briefcases and small wheels
And shutters drawn because it's winter
Because it's summer! And they're on holiday.
Because they're busy,
And the ferry is no longer running.

It's the blue from Senja just before sunrise
And all I can hear are waves and oyster catchers.
                 But it's dirty. It's a factory blue.

I'll spend my change on a beer. An hour's wages.
Wonder where it all ends up. Goes down some chute,
Gets counted, and then?
There are islands out there
The bastards have boats.

But there's plenty to look at.
The toilets are well marked.
The duty free sign is glowing red;
Money dumping ground.

Outside you'll have to follow the herd
To the allocated zones.

Angry Woodcutter in Ireland 2010

Feels like
Some days there's just a white line moving underneath you;
The sheep are solitary,
Rusty fence wire is camouflaged
Against heather,
There are piles of mouldy turf,
And ditches in the peat,
Where man and machine worked.

They've been away
But in a way it was
Home from home;
Where ever you go
There are the Irish.

You have to stand in the saddle for the broken stretches of road.
And when you stop
First for beer, then water,
They'll tell you – they always come home.

Rain falls in rods.
There are elms, willow scrub, buttercups, leaf mould.

The family that lived here,
Kept pigs and grew swedes
And potatoes.

System Updates Loading

Eyes which are poems
That take risks.
Candid. If that's possible.
Guarded if not.
Kind eyes.
Sad, selfless; sly?
Self conscious eyes
With a story behind them:
Passionate, wise
Human eyes.
I'm looking
But all I can see
Are screen savers.

My Turn

and suddenly everything was different
because a woman was standing against me
because the leaves were falling outside in the darkness
and my heart was beating like a caged bird
and I couldn't hear the wind
or feel her heart beating against mine
because of mine
trying to calm it, but not managing
because of her neck smell
because she was Jane Austen and I was holding her by the
waist
and my thoughts were spinning into nothing
and It was turning, following her
her one breast that stroked across me
I didn't know about the other
I was just concentrating on the one,
but when I leant back her eyes were blue And grey
and the skin inside her arm was cool.
Then suddenly everything was different
and I was wondering if, for her, this was all just a game...
but I knew, by her breath against my neck
and her delicate red ears

A Door Closes

And you're back in that game of croquet
with stupid people
lost in pursuit of happiness.

At least they're kind,
they don't have to be
like that, even that,
they're not paid to do it.

They just like to I suppose,
because it's nice to be nice,
it's good to have standards.

But anyway, back to the game
which never ends
until everyone's dropped out
and the winner wins a little statue.

Competition

At the party he explained
How trees in the forest grow tall and slender
Planted close together

They listened enrapt
As he told them his philosophy
It blew over them as they rocked -

"I don't believe in competition."
He said. "I believe in interaction, adaption, cooperation."

"That's competition." Someone suggested
The room was full and drinks were spilling.

"Then how do you explain." He said.
"When one falls they all fall
Dominoes into the hole made for them."

The people propping up the bar
Paid no attention. But they held the others in…

And then they danced. Danced and danced.
And some of them would have fallen
But others stopped them
And held them up, in their merriment
Their legs like those of stumbling puppets,
Shoulders held firmly amidst the shaking laughter.

And out in the darkness the trees creaked,
Their leaves brushed against each other
And rustled. It sounded like silk.

Later he stood alone
Like a solitary tree
Whose companions have long since returned to the earth
From which they came – sparring and jostling.

Out of this

(Conversations in India)

'Wasteland something must come;
Pioneers are always selfish, beautiful
but in a destructive way, fighting,
exposing hypocrisies...'
        'But it is not the system that fails them
or money or temptations
it is still themselves – competitive.'

'Love is not the problem it is attachment.'
And the Baba's eyes wander to where we sit,
And the Israeli with the fake fur is thinking
with his dick
'But if I am not attached to you I cannot love you.'
And the other Baba passes the chillum
'Shanti, shanti.'
'You cannot love me from a distance?'
And the other Israeli believes
love starts with the self,
wind blows snow off the mountain
more glacier breaks into the river
'No. I can think of you.
Until I know you I cannot love you.
It is inevitable you will have changed
since we last met.'
And the Babas blow smoke into the thin air

And the Israelis with their joints watch and learn
how the big smokers smoke
And the Chi shop man smiles
And the Babas with big beards walk down from the mountain
their robes blowing
and their feet subtle as smooth stones
          And the girl with the didgeridoo
plays her note

Send us a Postcard

I might have said:
Godspeed!
And take care
Yourself, watch for pitfalls,
Roll the tent when it's hot.

Show trust, but hold a bit back
Don't worry about the biological imperative –
It doesn't count unless it's love.

Don't think you're the only one –
Everyone else fucked it too

I said:
Send us a postcard.

Shooting Stars

I've been shooting stars –
After the first
"BANG"
Flight of rooks
And village silence
There is nothing
But a black space
In a cloudless sky.

I've been shooting cars –
After the
"PCHOOoooooo"
And crack of metal against metal
There is nothing
But the smell of burning.

Before long
The sky is cloudless, moonless
And black.
And the river as quiet
As a fractured rock –
Not even blood could claim it.

And I feel nothing.

What led to being Caught?

You were bowling along thinking of other things,
coasting into the thirty zone,
on a downhill road, deceptive,
snaking through the village.
      It was dry. Everyone in the world
was speeding.

These are all linked to speed.
Speeds are reducing,
again they're painted orange, and
there's a significant trend
to take a chance
if you know you're not gonna get done.
      but it's an absolute offense
it could cause a crash, everybody knows that
things get a bit misleading -
that's when to take the slow down approach.

It's all related to speed.
Don't be fooled. There might be one
that's fallen out of the criteria,
don't be fooled by that one.
think outside the box
because that's where the clusters tend to occur
      just when your concentration lapses
           think about the calibration lines -
all related to speed.

Just when you think you've eliminated all your options
change your thinking slightly - don't take a chance;
life kicks in, it's all about averages -
don't be fooled by averages.

So. You're now driving solo.
Bolt on an extra little bit of information
and highlight it – there might be something physical -
And remember
It all happens at the end of the braking pattern.

All these things are distractions,
patterns of behaviour.
        There are people walking dogs! It's interesting...
it's about being aware, and responsible.
        And what about the pedestrian?   Pedestrians take
priority.

Ode to a Pair of Boots

Soles worn
uppers split
big hole at base of big toe left
right uppers shot through at ankle
inards collapsing
toe caps parting
leather thin, cracked
Polish leather
or Russian.

Roof of Reeds

It was the way he spoke that first
I couldn't follow what he said
I wasn't concentrating
There was a girl
And I wondered.

He spoke beautifully
As if he was
Totally without
Saying it like
I can't
But it was amazing
It really was
Everyone thought so
They knew

We're Most Worried About You

Followed by anyone who arrives on the scene.
Make sure things are being done properly.
Morally very difficult. But, first
You <u>have to</u>: assess the situation.
For this use all your senses – listening, observing,
Smelling... This could include behind doors,
Up and down. If there's a hole
You could go down it too.

If there's blood coming from his head it's a head injury.
      There's a huge spectrum of illness.
The casualty will do most of the primary survey for you.
Don't strip them. It's manipulating underwear
That sort of stuff.
You're all aware we should be reporting near misses.:

After two minutes you shouldn't be completely exhausted.
Ask yourself this: is it a good response?
Sometimes they might just talk nonsense,
Or they might be unresponsive. Remember:
The smallest person can do this to the biggest person.

The initial response is usually quite emotional
Due to the chaotic electrical activity in the brain.
That's why we don't restrain.

Where we Meet

He knew that I knew he was robbing me,
candidly, he knew

That when two men meet
out of the dust
that switches through the door, and
sprawls into continents:
padded over,
belched into,
whisked up and driven
into small storms,
Gathered.

And the cranky thing
squeaks open.
And the dust flies in like a spawning.
Until all settles
        when
there are two men
sitting.

He wasn't to know that I never haggle
that I think haggling sucks
pitch it right and respect – that's the game.
    I wasn't to know that he weren't a high starter
      When

We weren't to know that something timeless
and historic could happen – cross cultural,
intelligent
      That
In a moment.

Machine Strike

I know I'm not supposed to answer back
with more questions.
I know my role is to eject
good things when you press buttons.
I know I have chips on all sides
from where you keep dropping me
on concrete platforms;
I am full of imitation coins
and stale food
and unhoped for sex.
        But, ladies and gentlemen, this machine
is full of money and other treasure.
        But boys and girls all the buttons
are now jammed, the key slots
have matches in them
and no amount of punching
or other demonstrations of displeasure
will get it out.
Not even silence.
Remember, this machine is well practiced at that.

Another Casablanca Moment

I knew it was just another ploy:
He was depressed you said
he's lost you, I'd be depressed
then I realised
what you were really saying was:
'I have to go to him.'
then everything made sense;
It was karma and I should be glad of it,
history repeats itself until you realise
sometimes you've got to make a decision for someone
because they can't.
      'You're getting on that plane.' I'd have said,
but there was no plane so I didn't say anything.

A Little Recipe

First take a little dignity
mix it with humility.
Then give credence
to honour, and add a generous helping
of duty and responsibility.
Stir with love,
allow to simmer gently
with humour.
Share out equally.

I was at the Bar

I'd ordered and was waiting for a mate
when this bird walks in wearing
silver
walks straight past all the monkeys at the door
and the smart dudes at the end of the bar
near the till where the waitresses flitted in and out
like sparrows
came straight over
sat herself down
don't get me wrong
I've seen all the films too:
I'd have loved to have acted the part
and said the few words one says
and felt the softness of her
and felt the giving of myself to her -
beauty and mutual blankness -
she as some girl
me as some guy
seizing the moment
would have been a lightening from something

but as it was it wasn't me but some code
she sat by – safe.
As it was it wasn't the man she sat by
the walking talking penis
the man monkey orgasm machine
the wandering male
the lost Y.
It was the dignified man made king!
The pure thing she made it her business to corrupt
to amuse herself by making something rigid bend -
what a trophy that could be
a man more than a man but the very code
to wear! To nestle in. To tease.

So there I sat. Some harbour!
If she'd but known the little I had
and how great the effort to keep it -
which gave the appearance of valour!
So there we sat, comfortably
her hated beauty
and my respect.

Also Chris Deakins: Chapbook 'In A Parallel World'
Published by original plus. 2011.

www.ingramcontent.com/pod-product-compliance
Lightning Source LLC
Chambersburg PA
CBHW060635030426
42337CB00018B/3369